ROMAN MANCETTER

COLIN BADDELEY
(1923 – 2012)

THE ATHERSTONE ARCHAEOLOGICAL
AND HISTORICAL SOCIETY (1907-2006)

Editors: Dr. Nigel Melton, Margaret Hughes,
Philip Taylor, Judy Vero

Atherstone Civic Society

2013

Published by Atherstone Civic Society

www.atherstonecivicsociety.co.uk

Email: secretary@atherstonecivicsociety.co.uk

© Atherstone Civic Society 2013

ISBN 978-0-9551803-1-6

Designed by Andy Mathias
Printed and bound in Great Britain

CONTENTS

ABOUT THE AUTHOR

A bank manager by profession, Colin Baddeley had a passion for Roman history and for many years was part of the excavation team of Atherstone Archaeological and Historical Society which carried out a number of digs in and around Mancetter under their director, Keith Scott. The article which he contributed to *Current Archaeology* in 1991 (issue no.125) demonstrates his commitment to promoting the Roman Mancetter findings to a wider audience. He noted with prescience that "Mancetter has proved to be a site of major importance".

Colin became an expert on Roman coins and also conducted a number of tours of the Moselle Valley where wine-tasting was combined with Roman history. He died in 2012.

FOREWORD

This book on Roman Mancetter and Witherley could not have been written were it not for the work of archaeologists over many years. The fortified road station on the Watling Street, in the vicinity of The Bull, was excavated by Bryan O'Neill in the 1920s, Adrian Oswald in the 1950s, and Christine Mahany in the 1960s[1]. Kay Hartley, the country's authority on the *mortarium*, the ubiquitous Roman kitchen mixing bowl, carried out excavations on several sites in the area. In particular, in a series of annual campaigns, she examined the whole of the large field known as the Broad Close. Lastly, but not in the least, is the Society's own Keith Scott. Among Keith's many excavation projects were those for Roman tile and pottery kilns; he was also involved in a number of medieval pottery kiln excavations: Chilvers Coton, Nuneaton, for example. His crowning achievement, however, was his enormous contribution to our understanding of the mid-first century military history of the Midlands, by virtue of his work on the half-legionary fortress at Mancetter, ably supported by a dedicated digging team.

[1] References, Appendix 5

Keith had always hoped to locate and excavate a Roman masonry building, and in 1996, three years before his death, having been called in by the farmer when the plough turned up brick, tile and plaster, he had the evidence to recognise the existence of such a building. He was granted sufficient time in the following year to mount a trial

excavation which revealed the foundations of a portion of it. A comment he made during the dig was: "Trust me to find a villa at this time of my life!"

INTRODUCTION

The origin of this project lies in the decision of the Atherstone Archaeological Society to mount a series of guided walks around Roman Mancetter in the late 1980s, to enable interested members of the public, and other archaeological societies, to become aware of the importance of Roman Mancetter. The suggestion was made by Keith Scott, who, with myself as Chairman, led the walks. It became clear that 'handouts' were needed and these expanded in content as the 'Roman Trail' became popular. My successor as Chairman of the Society, Philip Taylor, encouraged me to increase the written contents and to add an account of the Boudican Revolt; he also continued the trail walks as leader.

From a personal point of view, due to major health problems affecting my wife, the drafts of the Roman Mancetter text have lain untouched for a number of years. However, I have been motivated to bring the project forward again, and after a complete revision of the contents, here it is.

Colin Baddeley
2008

Map 1

ROMAN BRITAIN
Schematic map of primary military
roads, post invasion of AD 43

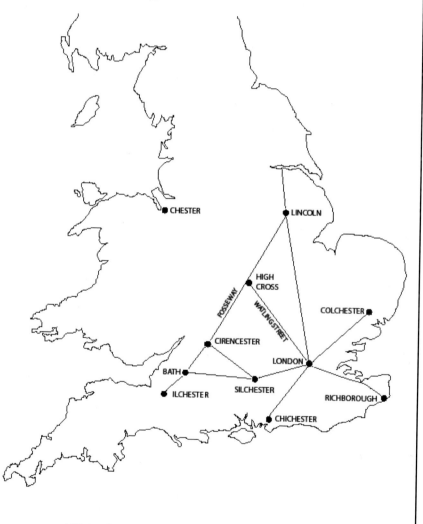

N.B. Modern places names included for location purposes.

CHAPTER 1 - THE
HISTORICAL BACKGROUND

In AD 43, during the reign of the Emperor Claudius, a Roman army landed in Kent and the incorporation of Britain into the Roman Empire had begun. The commander-in-chief was Aulus Plautius, his force comprising four legions plus auxiliary regiments of infantry and cavalry, a total of some fifty thousand men. The work of the Roman navy must not be overlooked in this operation; it was indeed the equivalent for its time of the 1944 D-Day invasion of Normandy. It is estimated that the Roman army would have needed up to a thousand ships for the transportation of troops, horses and supplies, and would have required re-supply following the successful landing.

Plautius defeated the British tribal levies under their commanders Caratacus and Togidumnus. The latter was killed, and Caratacus fled west. The Emperor himself came to Britain with an entourage including elephants, and received the surrender of eleven British tribes at *Camulodunum* (Colchester) the tribal capital of a major tribe, the *Catuvellauni*. Aulus Plautius was appointed the first governor of the new province, the capital being established at *Camulodunum*. This civil area initially covered what are simply the lowlands of England, namely the Midlands, the south and the east, although, Rome implied that it was the whole of *Britannia*.

The governor's immediate tasks were the establishment of the civil administration, and the setting-up of a tax collection system – bureaucracy never changes throughout the ages! He also needed to deploy troops for garrison duties throughout the territory under Roman control, which implied much fort and road construction by the army. Treaty arrangements were concluded with certain tribes who agreed to accept the role of client kingdoms.[2] It must also be recalled that the second legion under its legate Vespasian continued to be engaged in operations against the *Durotriges* in the southwest.

The Fosse Way (as it later became known) was constructed as part of the military roads programme and at this stage provided a route linking the Bristol Channel area and the Humber estuary, forming a *limes* (pronounced 'lee-maze').

The Latin word *limes* at this period was used to describe a military road functioning as a link connecting a series of military posts. This implies that the Fosse was not a defensive frontier; it is best viewed as the boundary between the area of civil administration and the military zone.

---

[2] "A client-king was a local ruler friendly to Rome, whose loyalty bought a measure of independence from heavy-handed colonial authority". Aldhouse-Greene, *Boudica Britannia* (page 7), Pearson Education Ltd, 2006. See also Chapter 5, pages 53-54

To the west of the Fosse there was certainly a military presence, with out-posted troops in forts. The area would have been patrolled, and cavalry used for this task, as well as infantry. We are perhaps visualising an area with a depth of twenty to thirty miles (32 to 48 kilometres). Interestingly, there was some slight evidence at Mancetter for activity pre-dating the main occupation, but this was found at one point only, during the excavations on the south side of the later legionary fortress. It may date to this period under discussion.

To the northwest lay the extensive tribal area of the *Brigantes*, who, under their pro-Roman Queen Cartimandua, were in a treaty arrangement with Rome as a client kingdom. The tribal area covered much of Yorkshire and Lancashire and as far north as the River Tyne. The tribal centre lay at Stanwick St. John, halfway between Darlington and Barnard Castle. The enormous earthworks stretching for miles are highly visible. The presence of this pro-Roman kingdom ensured the safety of the province to the north.

Aulus Plautius retired during the winter of AD 47/48 and his replacement Ostorius Scapula was immediately faced with a major problem. It seems probable that Caratacus seized the opportunity offered by the change in Governor to lead an incursion of free British and Welsh tribes into the new province. This was defeated and the invaders driven back, but it was clear that the Fosse Way *limes* had no further role to play. In order to control the

Welsh tribes etc., Scapula's solution was to move the military zone forward to the western edge of the Severn Valley, and a series of forts was established to control the valleys leading into the Welsh foothills. The area became known many centuries later as The Welsh Marches.

This reorganisation commenced in AD 48/49 and we now see the construction of a substantial military base at Mancetter by the fourteenth legion. The second legion was already based in the south, possibly at Alchester, Oxfordshire (where evidence has emerged recently of a half-legionary type fortress) and the ninth legion at Longthorpe near Peterborough. Mancetter and Longthorpe were of the half-legionary type. (See Chapter 2.) The twentieth legion was moved from *Camulodunum* to a full-size fortress at Gloucester, sited at Kingsholm. The second legion may well have been moved into the Dorset area at this time or even earlier as its campaign in the southwest continued.

The pacification of the Welsh tribes was continued by the two governors who succeeded Ostorius Scapula. Tacitus tells us that Scapula "died, worn out with care". But he had succeeded in defeating Caratacus in a major battle, capturing his family. Although Caratacus himself evaded capture and escaped to the *Brigantes*, their Queen handed him over to Scapula. Caratacus and family were sent to Rome where Claudius showed clemency and there they lived out the rest of their natural lives in peace.

Map 2
ROMAN BRITAIN
Schematic map of the developing
military road system circa AD 55-60

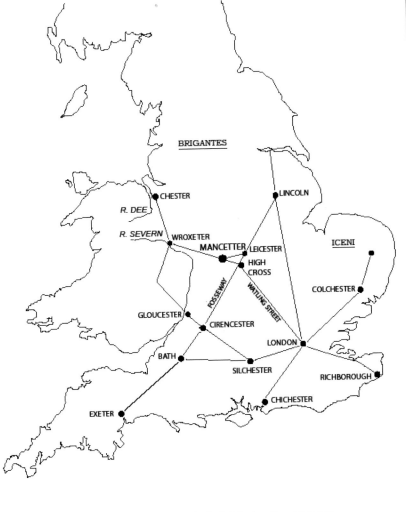

N.B. Modern places names included for location purposes.

During AD 54 Claudius died, probably murdered, and Nero became Emperor. It became his policy to pursue much more aggressively the pacification of the Welsh tribes, and it was at this time the decision was made to move the fourteenth legion forward from Mancetter. Dr. Graham Webster considered that the construction of the full size legionary fortress at Wroxeter, near Shrewsbury, was commenced circa AD 56/58. Indeed, this may have coincided with the arrival in the province of the next governor, C. Suetonius Paulinus in AD 58. Mancetter was evacuated and dismantled. Military control was also imposed in the extensive area to the north of Shrewsbury up to the Dee and Mersey estuaries, forts being established. It seems probable that the later legionary fortress site at Chester was included in these arrangements. The second legion also seems likely to have moved forwards to Exeter in this period.

For two years Paulinus conducted highly successful campaigns into Wales, and in AD 60 mounted his attack on the druidic centre of Anglesey. Whilst so engaged, he, and indeed Rome, were faced with an unprecedented crisis in Britain: the Boudican revolt.

The Watling Street[3] itself was originally constructed as a military road to link London with the Fosse Way as it passes through the Midlands heading for Leicester and beyond to the Humber. The Roman name is unknown – indeed no name is known for any road in Britain.

[3]"It was called by the Anglo-Saxons Wæclinga stræt or Wætlinga stræt in the late 9th century, that is 'Roman road of the Wæclingas (the family or followers of a man called *Wæcel)'." *A Dictionary of British Place Names* A. D. Mills, OUP, 2011

16

Where the Watling Street meets the Fosse a small town developed known as *Venonis*. This is the modern High Cross. Consequently, upon the relocation of the army into the Severn Valley in the late fifties, the Watling Street was extended to Wroxeter and beyond.

The earliest evidence for a Roman presence in the Mancetter area is provided by an air photograph taken by the late James Pickering. The photograph shows the line of the ditch on all four sides of a military encampment lying mainly in the field next to that known as the Broad Close, down almost to the River Anker. During the excavations of the pottery

Aerial photograph showing crop mark of marching camp (drawn over in red as original photograph badly faded).

manufacturing site in the Broad Close a small section of this ditch was revealed.

It was recognised as being military, but could not be followed up as it was close to the field boundary. However, it can now be placed in a proper context. The encampment was clearly of a temporary nature, and was probably a marching camp relating to the earliest army penetration of the area. A work camp is another possibility. (See Chapter 4 page 51).

Map 3

THE VILLAGE OF MANCETTER

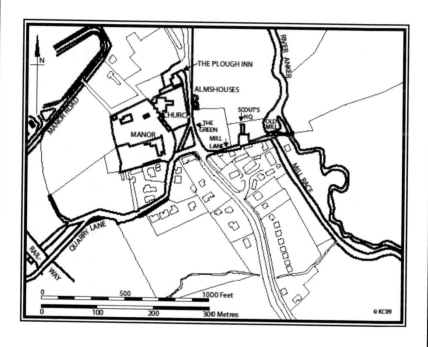

Mancetter – the name

It is not known when the settlement and *burgus* lying on the Watling Street at Mancetter/Witherley was given its Roman name of *Manduessedum*. It appears in the Antonine Itinerary, a third century compilation of approximately two hundred routes, complete with place names, covering the whole of the Roman Empire. Certainly the name must have been in use much earlier, but it is doubtful if it would have been given during the mid-first century military phase. The name is formed of two components: the British Celtic *mandu* meaning small horse or pony, and *essedo*, borrowed early from Celtic Gaul into Latin, meaning war chariot, a wheeled vehicle, or even just a cart.[4] One possibility would be the early establishment of a *mansio*, a posting station similar to that at Wall near Lichfield. A Roman 'motel' would be another useful description. These are found at intervals on all major Roman roads and provided accommodation, usually bathing facilities, and a change of horses.

[4]For more information see *The Place Names of Roman Britain*, Rivet & Smith, B.T. Batsford, 1979

19

CHAPTER 2 - THE
LEGIONARY FORTRESS

On the ridge where now stands Mancetter Church and the Manor
(OS grid ref. SP 320 967) lay the fortress constructed in AD 49/50
by the fourteenth legion, *Legio XIV Gemina*. This is a superb
defensive position. To the east the ground falls sharply away to
the River Anker; to the south it slopes down to a brook, a tributary
of the Anker. On the western side lies the valley through which
runs the canal and railway, and to the north, although not very
apparent due to modern housing, the ground falls gently away
towards Atherstone. Constructed in timber and with a turf and
timber rampart, the fortress occupied an area of approximately
twenty-eight acres (11 hectares) and had four gateways.

A full size legionary fortress was approximately fifty acres (20
hectares) and the preferred description for one of the Mancetter
type is a 'half legionary fortress'. The term 'vexillation fortress'
is also sometimes used although, strictly speaking, 'vexillation'
implies the brigading together of units of both legionary and
auxiliary troops. When at least half the men are out-posted or on
campaign there is no point in constructing a full size establishment.

Half legionary fortresses are a known feature of the Roman army;
and were the headquarters of the respective legions following the
invasion of AD 43.

Map 4

MANCETTER:
THE HALF-LEGIONARY
FORTRESS SITE

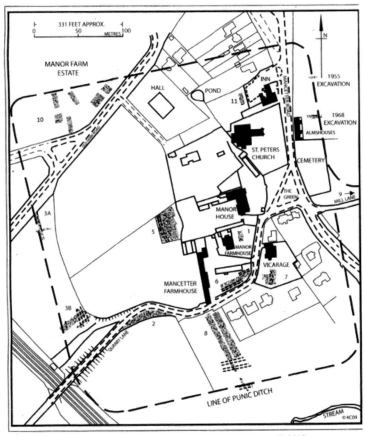

331 FEET APPROX.
0   50   100
        METRES

MANOR FARM
ESTATE

HALL

POND

INN

1955
EXCAVATION

1968
EXCAVATION

ALMSHOUSES

10

11

ST. PETERS
CHURCH

CEMETERY

THE
GREEN

9
MILL LANE

3A

5

MANOR
HOUSE

1

MANOR
FARMHOUSE

VICARAGE

MANCETTER
FARMHOUSE

6

7

38

2

8

QUARRY LANE

LINE OF PUNIC DITCH

STREAM

© KC09

N

LOCATIONS OF ARCHAEOLOGICAL EXCAVATIONS

AREA OF EXCAVATION =
DEFENSIVE DITCHES   =

SEE APPENDIX 4 FOR EXCAVATION SEQUENCE

However, the twentieth, *Legio XX*, was based in a full size legionary fortress at *Camulodunum* (Colchester), the capital of the province. *Legio XIV*, prior to Mancetter, was sited to the south of Northampton, evidence for which has only recently emerged. All were situated well to the rear of the Fosse military border zone. (It was policy not to locate a legionary headquarters actually on a frontier or border of this type).

Although finds of Roman material have been mentioned by antiquarian writers, the first indication of a Roman military fortress on the ridge at Mancetter was identified by Adrian Oswald in 1955[5].

Arrangements had been made by the then Ministry of Works for Birmingham Museum to observe and record the archaeology revealed by sewerage and gas main excavations in the *burgus* area during 1954/55, and Adrian Oswald, then the museum director, undertook the task, subsequently mounting three excavations to clarify points arising during the course of this work. Being aware of much earlier reports of occasional finds of Roman pottery, even a denarius of Vespasian recorded in 1622, he visited Mancetter village and noticed an earthwork forming a low bank turning a corner in the field neighbouring the Almhouses. Wondering if it were possible that this represented the vestiges of the corner of a defensive rampart, he trenched the earthwork only to find that

[5]References, Appendix 5

22

it was a medieval hedge bank. He realised, however, that the ground beneath showed evidence of having been disturbed, and continued with his excavation. This revealed a substantial Roman defensive ditch and in the bottom fill there was recovered a Samian rim sherd dated to the first century AD. This was from a decorated bowl made in southern Gaul (see Appendix 2).

A few years later in 1964[6] a drain was being laid in the vicinity of the original Manor gates giving access to The Green, and a small coin hoard was discovered with some undateable Roman pottery fragments. There were sixteen coins in all, including a silver denarius of the Republic, c.150-125 BC, another of the Emperor Tiberius dated to AD14-37, and an as of Augustus. The remainder, nine brass dupondii and four copper asses were all of the reign of Claudius. Although all the coins were corroded, those dated to Claudius are examples of copies made in Britain for use as small change by the army and civil administration – these were an official issue. It looks as though a soldier buried his savings for whatever reason and failed to retrieve them.

Excavations carried out over many years by the late Keith Scott, together with members of the Atherstone Archaeological and Historical Society, have provided a great deal of information on the details of construction of the fortress.

[6]For this and other archaeological references, see Appendix 5

The line of the rampart and defensive ditches – two inner, fronting the rampart, and a third lying much further out known as a 'punic' ditch[7] - have been revealed on all four sides. Internally, a major building was located, probably the headquarters building known as the *principia*. Several barrack blocks were also revealed. Also recovered was the evidence for a secondary phase fort, the site having been re-occupied by the army following the Boudican revolt. This was much smaller and given up during the last quarter of the first century. Small finds include pottery, coins, various bronze and other metal items. Fittings for legionary armour were also found, including fragments of the iron plates of the laminated cuirass, *lorica segmentata*. No gates have been excavated, but the positions of those on the east and west sides can be estimated with reasonable accuracy.

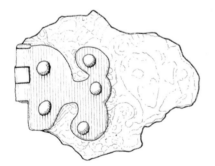

Drawing of a hinged part of a shoulder strap from Roman body armour, *lorica segmentata*, found close to Quarry Lane, Mancetter (*Birmingham & Warwickshire Archaeological Society, Transactions*, Vol 91, p.21)

No direct evidence confirming that the *Lego XIV Gemina* was based at Mancetter has been discovered, but towards the end of the AD fifties a new full size legionary fortress was constructed by

[7]Appendix 1 includes a description of a punic ditch

Legio XIV at Wroxeter near Shrewsbury. Since Mancetter was dismantled at the same time, it leads to the conclusion that it was occupied by the fourteenth legion. Dismantling involved levelling the ramparts by pushing the material into the ditches. Rubbish and anything unusable was also deposited therein or into latrine or water storage pits – indeed any other hole in the ground; this material all awaits the archaeologists' trowels. Re-usable timber was recovered and the rest burned, hence the frequent finds of burned clay from the wattle and daub construction of many of the buildings. Finally, the demolition party would leave the fort site cleared, tidy and vacant.

THE DEFENCES

In the field next to the almshouses mentioned earlier, an opportunity arose during 1968 which enabled Keith Scott and his team to put in a trial trench closer to the building. This located the same defensive ditch found by Oswald, together with a second, inner, ditch, and at last it was possible to demonstrate the line of the eastern defences of the fortress.

From The Green next to the church, Mill Lane dips down to the River Anker. The east gate of the fortress lies roughly where the lane meets the main road. Down the lane on the left-hand side is the new Scout Centre, and prior to the foundations being put in and the car park being surfaced, Keith Scott mounted excavations that proved extremely helpful in gaining more of an understanding of the fort. On the wall opposite is a plaque placed there by the Archaeological Society, recording his findings, together with the rest of the fort perimeter. There had long been a problem with respect to the inner two ditches of the fort and the outer punic ditch, as to what happened in the Almshouses section of the ditches. Also, the work that was carried out at the time of the redevelopment of the Scout Centre in the mid-1990s showed that the outer punic ditch came in much closer to the two inner ditches, and all three (a most unusual feature) turned down towards the River Anker as they approached the position of the east gate. This is shown quite clearly on the plaque. In addition to this information regarding the line of the fort ditches, four deep pits/wells were located close to the line of the access road leading from the east gate to the River Anker crossing.

In one, probably a well, preserved in the water-logged conditions was a remarkable discovery: two worked planks. The length of each was approximately thirty-six inches (90 cms), but each was broken into two pieces under the weight of the pit fill. Dendrochronological examination has dated the planks to the mid-first century AD. Also recovered was a wooden bowl very well preserved after two thousand years in the well.

Wooden bowl from Mill Lane excavation
(courtesy of Warwickshire Museum)

In another pit, to the excavator's surprise, were the bones of four dogs. Inevitably, in the general area of the excavations, Roman pottery sherds were recovered and one complete small vessel. Of coins there were a dupondius and, remarkably, an Iron Age gold half-stater of the nearby *Coritani* tribe. Also found were five rare terra-cotta loom weights[8].

Loom weight from
Mill Lane excavation

Metal items included two fragments of gilded bronze alloy that may represent the remains of decorative embellishment on a sword or dagger scabbard. There was a similar find made in the fort interior during one of the excavations in the 1980s.

Having discussed the eastern defences and the position of the gate, mention now needs to be made of the other three sides of the fortress. The western defences were the subject of three research excavations during the 1980s when the ditch system (two inner ditches and an outer punic) was clearly revealed. In the early 1990s two substantial trenches were put in on the southern side, again establishing the line of the ditch system. The most difficult to locate was on the northern side, as this was obscured by a housing estate. When a number of houses in the vicinity of Farm Road

[8]This find was not included in the writer's typescript and has been added by the editor.

were demolished and rebuilt in recent years, the opportunity was taken to excavate and the defensive ditches were found. They proved to be slightly further to the north than expected, but at last it was now possible to establish the actual size of the fortress – twenty-eight acres (11 hectares).

Immediately past the main gates of Mancetter Manor, in Quarry Lane, is a drive to a house along which is a Victorian gas lamp. In the 1970s, the then owner of the property, Dr. Brian Kelham, wishing to embellish the drive as well as provide illumination, was digging a hole in which to install the lamp. In doing so he found the tops of two large pots. He called in Keith Scott, who continued with the excavation. What had been discovered was a small cellar associated with the centurions' quarters of a Roman barrack block. Inside and still standing, leaning against the cellar side (planking

Dr. Brian Kelham with one of the *amphorae* found in his garden.

or wattle long gone), were two *amphorae*, one complete and another almost complete. *Amphorae* were used for the importation of olive oil and wine.

28

In view of the importance, Keith obtained Dr. Kelham's permission to excavate the neighbouring lawn hoping to recover the barrack block, only to find that it lay in the opposite direction and was impossible to reach. However, this was still an important dig since, sealed by a Roman gravel surface, an important find was made, namely a piece of plate armour, *lorica segmentata*[9]. This could only have been from legionary armour and makes it certain that legionaries were present at Mancetter.

A few metres further up Quarry Lane, where it makes a sharp right hand bend, on the left stands the new vicarage. When the foundations were laid, a number of Roman features were recorded in the sides of the trenches. Finds included a coin, Samian and other pottery, amongst which was a 'graffito pot' with the owner's name, 'BIILALVCI' (Belalucius) scratched on it.

Drawing of graffito (*Birmingham & Warwickshire Archaeological Society, Transactions*, Vol 102, p.24)

Opposite the vicarage lies a grassed area, once a farm yard with associated buildings. All are now residential and much changed since Keith Scott and his excavating team carried out a major research excavation there in the 1980s. Virtually the whole of

[9]See page 24 .

the area between the houses and the road was excavated over two years. Here lay evidence for the construction of the AD 48/49 fortress and its demolition when the *Legio XIV Gemina* was moved forward yet again in the late AD fifties to Wroxeter, there to construct its new base. The post-Boudica re-occupation of the site after AD 61 was also identified. This was an auxiliary fort, of approximately seven acres (3 hectares), which in turn was given up later in the century, perhaps in the AD eighties, when a military presence in the Midlands was no longer necessary, the army being engaged in operations in the north of England and Scotland.

Among all the evidence for buildings and features was one of outstanding interest. It lay, indeed still lies, close to the bend in the road, deep underground. It consists of a long stone-built flue containing much soot and charcoal and, when fully excavated, had a stone-filled drain in the bottom. At the termination of the flue, the 'business end', lay a circular chamber, but it was not a kiln. A fragment of bronze sheet was found among the evidence of burning in the bottom of the

The "mystery feature" on Site 6. "This kiln had a very long flue, and a lot of charcoal, but little evidence for high temperatures. Was it a cauldron for heating water?" (Baddeley: *'Current Archaeology' No. 125.*)

30

chamber, which was about five feet (1.5 metres) in diameter. The purpose of the installation is uncertain but one possibility advanced by the excavator is that it was designed to heat water in some quantity. Unfortunately, the stoke hole which may have provided more information lies under the road, and is impossible to access.

In rubbish pits relating to the demolition of the fortress were found a number of small but important objects. These included lamps, one of which was intact; a coin of Vespasian, little worn; a broken pot that had contained paint which was still adhering to the sherds; and in the same pit was a small quantity of paint pigments. Probably the most exciting of all the material were three so-called 'eye-ball' beads no larger than a small finger nail. These were provenanced by the country's leading expert on ancient beads, Margaret Guido, to the north shore of the Black Sea, beyond the frontier of the Empire.

Picture Lamp from Quarry Lane excavation

Coin of Vespasian found at Quarry Lane

Eye beads found at Quarry Lane

The southern defences of the fortress were found south of Quarry Lane, beyond the village. A large field dips away to a brook at its bottom. Keith Scott and his team mounted a large excavation in order to trace the position of these defences. The excavation consisted of two very substantial trenches.

Whilst it is difficult to understand the situation now, the rampart and inner ditches lie about half way down the field, perhaps ten yards (9 nine metres) beyond the existing fence. The punic ditch was discovered by using a small excavating machine moving down the field until the ditch was located[10]. The inner ditches were excavated completely and evidence was found for the turf and timber rampart. In the year in

Punic ditch, from south of Quarry Lane

which the excavations took place, the site was flown over by Jim Pickering and for the first time the line of the defences was evident from the air.

In addition to locating the defences much evidence was also recovered for internal buildings and the demolition and subsequent reoccupation. A pit which pre-dated the Roman buildings contained a quantity of charred grain.

[10]Appendix 1 includes a description of a punic ditch

The half-sectioned pit with a layer of charred cereal grain in its base, found on Site 8, the southern defences of the fortress. This pre-Roman pit has been cut by the 'U-shaped' foundation slot of a building from the early Roman fortress.

Further along Quarry Lane, on the left-hand bend, road widening was undertaken in 1976, and during the course of the earth removal a large pit was uncovered. Keith Scott, realising that it was probably Roman, undertook the systematic excavation of the feature. This turned out to be a military latrine pit and in the bottom lay a quantity of pottery, most of it intact. There were six two-handled flagons all of the same style plus three small jars of differing style and size. The excavator wondered if they had been standing on a shelf which had given way and allowed the pottery to slip gently into the pit. Military latrine pits were not cess-pits. Buckets were placed in them below the 'fly level' and fatigue parties disposed of the contents regularly outside the fort.

Across the road, on the bend, is an old lane that runs down to the railway. This is a section of the original Quarry Lane as it was before the bridge was built and when the railway level crossing was in operation. The crossing keeper's house is still there. Immediately beyond the old lane, Keith Scott and his team carried out a major research excavation to find the western defences of the fortress. They determined the position of the rampart, which can be seen in a hedge bank on the right hand side. Then, in sequence, running down the field in the direction of the railway, the positions of the two inner ditches and the outer punic ditch were established and fully excavated. Further across the field towards the Old Farm Road housing estate, but diverging from the hedge, the punic ditch was twice located and fully excavated.

Group of two-handled flagons, and jars (front row) found at Quarry Lane

INTERNAL BUILDINGS

Next, permission was obtained from the then owner of Mancetter Manor to mount a further research excavation, during the course of which the whole of the old kitchen garden area was examined. This provided important information on the fortress interior. In particular, part of the site of the *principia*, the headquarters building, was revealed. The evidence consisted of very substantial foundation trenches packed with clay in which the nine-inch (23cm) square uprights had left their impression showing as dark patches, regularly spaced. This building was overlain by an uncompleted

The *principia* foundations in the Manor kitchen garden (Site 5). Colin Baddeley is seen close to a backfilled Saxo-Norman feature (marked by the bucket).

granary from a later fort. Much else was found, including a very large post-Roman storage pit with the stains of the timber lining perfectly clear. This was dated to the Saxo-Norman period. There was also evidence interpreted as from an initial, tented, phase of Roman occupation.

It did not prove possible to trace the *principia* further than the boundary hedge, since on the other side the ground level had been much lowered in Victorian times to create a tennis court.

Finally, no other archaeological excavations within the fortress have been carried out, except for an area excavated in 1984 prior to house construction on Nuneaton Road and work on the site of a new building at the Manor by Warwickshire Field Archaeology Unit. The whole site is, of course, scheduled by English Heritage, and any further work, if any, remains for the future.

Artist's impression of *principia* building at centre of half-legionary fortress. This provided a large space to address the men and offices for the executive requirements of the legion (*Photo Richard Haigh, courtesy of Friends of Atherstone Heritage*).

Map 5

Mancetter Village, Showing the *Burgus*

Also the outline of crop marks
See aerial photograph page 17

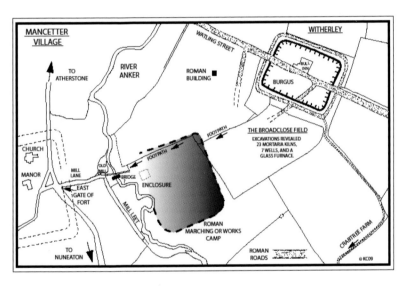

1. THE ENCLOSURE IN THE VICINITY OF THE FOOTBRIDGE ACROSS THE RIVER ANKER DATES CONCURRENTLY WITH THE FORTRESS. THERE WOULD ALSO HAVE BEEN A ROMAN BRIDGE OR FORD CROSSING THE RIVER.

2. THE ROMAN CAMP, IDENTIFIED FROM AIR PHOTOGRAPHY, UNDOUBTABLY PREDATES ALL OTHER FEATURES.

3. THE PLAN IS BASED ON EARLY ORDNANCE SURVEY MAPPING.

CHAPTER 3 - THE *BURGUS*

The Bull Inn at Witherley lies within a large rectangular enclosure, the *burgus*, through the middle of which passes Watling Street. Excavations, notably by O'Neill in 1927, Oswald in 1953-6, and Mahany[11] in 1964, have revealed a

Aerial photograph of burgus (*by courtesy of the Cambridge Collection of Air Photographs.*)

substantially constructed fortification with a stone wall some ten feet (3 metres) thick, enclosing an area of 1,200 by 800 feet (365 x 245 metres). The wall was backed by a clay rampart. Externally there was a double ditch system, the inner one being eighteen feet (5.50 metres) wide and nine feet (2.75 metres) deep. There were two gateways, their position still marked by the point where the Watling Street passes through the encampment on the short sides. The line of much of the wall and rampart, and the inner ditch, are clearly visible at the Bull Inn, and also in the field on the other side of the highway.

[11]References Appendix 5.

On the north side of the car parking area of The Bull, across the grass, are the buried remains of the wall, and beyond, dipping away sharply, lies the defensive ditch system. Although it is a double ditch, this is not obvious as it is overgrown. The line of the eastern wall is marked by the hedge running up to the road. In the other direction, the western side of the *burgus* is not clear, but Hunt Lane, running northwards at a right angle from Watling Street, may well follow the ditches.

In 1975[12] Keith Scott and his team carried out an excavation at the point where Watling Street crosses the River Anker to the west of The Bull. Here they found the Roman road and also a roadside ditch. It was found to be of two periods and contained pottery, some ironwork and a trumpet brooch.

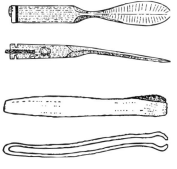

Then in 1993/4 a further excavation at Witherley Lodge on the north side of Watling Street, just to the west of the *burgus*, revealed first to third century AD activity in the form of a ditch, pit, and building. An intriguing find was part of a set of surgeon's instruments. There was also the base of a jar with the owner's name, 'SIIN' (Sen) scratched on to it[13].

Drawings of the copper alloy scalpel and tweezers found beside Watling Street at Witherley in 1993. (*Birmingham & Warwickshire Archaeological Society, Transactions*, Vol 112, p.40)

[12]References Appendix 5.

[13]These last two paragraphs were inserted by editor Nigel Melton.

On the opposite side of the Watling Street from The Bull, through a gate, is the access road leading to Crabtree Farm. The metalled track roughly follows the rampart line with the ditches on the right. It then curves sharply left to pick up the line of the western defences. The track continues to follow the line approximately, and the ditch system on the right is clearly evident. Looking ahead, eastwards, the line of the hedge in the distance continues to follow the rampart and the rise towards the main road and the position of the gate is distinctive.

What was the purpose of this substantial defensive structure, which incidentally had a relatively short life?

To answer this question we must go back to the reign of the emperor Diocletian, AD 285-305. He realised soon after his accession that the government and defence of such a vast empire were beyond the capabilities of one man, and introduced a series of reforms. The Empire was divided into two halves with joint emperors, each having prime responsibility for one half. Diocletian took charge of the East and Maximian the West. Each emperor, or Augustus, had a junior colleague (a sort of crown prince), termed a Caesar. Constantius was the Caesar of the West, and Galerius of the East. This arrangement is known as the Tetrarchy.

In AD 287, Carausius, commander of the channel fleet, rebelled, took over Britain and declared himself emperor of a breakaway state. Six years later and having until then defeated all attempts to recover the province by central government, Carausius was murdered and succeeded by his chief minister Allectus. It was a situation which had to be determined by Rome. Constantius, Caesar of the West, having captured Boulogne, which was held by the breakaway regime, brought an army to Britain in AD 296, defeated the forces of Allectus and reunited the province with the Empire. Constantius found the province in a state of chaos. Immediate action was needed to re-establish Imperial authority, and of prime importance was the creation of secure bases for the army along the important communications route of the Watling Street. Even so, the chain would have taken several years to complete, but a useful date is around AD 300; i.e. the very early fourth century.

Along this road between London and Wroxeter in Shropshire are located a number of similar fortifications, all built during this short period of time, all substantial defensive structures, as was the Mancetter *burgus*. The nearest of these strong points to Mancetter are *Letocetum* (Wall), near Lichfield, Staffordshire, a distance of sixteen miles (26 kilometres), and *Tripontium*, (Caves Inn), near Rugby, some nineteen miles (31 kilometres) away. Between Mancetter and Caves Inn there also lies the crossing of the Fosse Way and the Watling Street with a Roman township thereon named *Venonis*, now High Cross. No evidence for a *burgus* has so far been recovered there, although excavations have taken place and both civilian and some military activity has been found.

Map 6

MANCETTER'S
BURGUS

in relation to similar fortifications
along Watling Street.

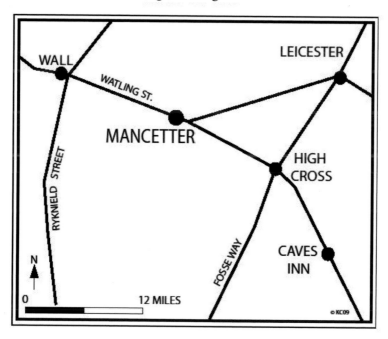

	ROMAN NAME
MANCETTER -	MANDUESSEDUM
WALL -	LETOCETUM
HIGH CROSS -	VENONIS
CAVES INN -	TRIPONTIUM
LEICESTER -	RATAE CORITANORUM

During the excavations at Mancetter (mentioned above), earlier second and third century occupation evidence was discovered underlying the *burgus*. A link road from the Watling Street giving access to the pottery manufacturing area (see Chapter Four) was destroyed by the construction of the *burgus's* southern defences. This link was replaced by a new road outside the western gateway of the encampment. Clearly the *burgus* was built on land cleared of earlier buildings as a matter of military policy. Assessment of the pottery finds and their stratification has led to a date being established of construction in the very early fourth century. No evidence of any permanent structure in the interior was found relating to its construction or use.

Constantius was elevated to Emperor of the Western half of the Empire on May 1st AD305, and almost immediately was involved again in Britain repelling an invasion by the Picts. He was at York when he died on July 25th AD 305. His son Constantine, who had been with him on campaign, was popular with the army in Britain and was hailed Emperor by the troops. The history of the years following is very complicated but by AD 324 Constantine I became the sole Augustus of the re-united Western and Eastern halves of the Empire. Constantine the Great, as he is known, was responsible for the Edict of Milan in AD 313 granting complete religious toleration to the peoples of the Empire, and is looked on as the first Christian Emperor.

Furthermore it was he who rebuilt Byzantium as the Christian capital of the Empire. The new city was formally dedicated on May 11th AD 330 and renamed Constantinopolis. Constantine the Great died on May 22nd AD 337.

CHAPTER 4 - BROAD CLOSE FIELD AND THE HARTSHILL/ MANCETTER POTTERY INDUSTRY

From the Watling Street opposite the Bull Inn, Witherley, the sign-posted field path leads south-west off the access road leading to Crabtree Farm and along the hedge to the north-west of the Broad Close. (See Map 5, page 37)

Mortarium (Kate Clarke)

Although other pot was made, especially in the early period, the main production was concerned with the kitchen mixing bowl called a *mortarium* (plural *mortaria*). A *mortarium* – even a small sherd – is instantly identifiable by what is known as the trituration grits on the interior. These are pounded-up tiny fragments of hard stone, e.g. river pebbles, flint and hard fired brick, (frequently a secondary use for broken tile). The fragments were pressed into the thrown pot before the clay had hardened prior to firing. The other identification features are a hooked rim for convenient holding, and a spout. The internal grits provide an abrasion - resistant surface. During the second century AD and up to circa AD 185, manufacturers placed a name stamp on the heavy rims. Considerable research has taken place, which in many cases enables *mortaria* experts to give a date of manufacture within a decade or two, and the place or area where the pottery was made. One such manufacturer was Sarrius, who came to Mancetter from an earlier location in southern England circa AD 130 and was in production until AD 170/180. Of his *mortaria*, over one hundred have been recovered in archaeological excavations throughout the Midlands, the north of England and even in Scotland where there was an army presence. In addition, over one hundred and twenty have been found as wasters in the Hartshill/Mancetter area. With the expansion of production in the late second century, a simplified rim form was developed by the potters and rim stamping ceased. Although Sarrius has been used as an example, there were many more potters working in our area over two centuries. Other important names are Marinus and Doccas.

The *mortarium* was introduced into the Roman world from Greece and rapidly became the standard 'food processor' in Italy and throughout the Empire as it expanded. Production was soon established by potters in the new provinces, often by migrating craftsmen, though the indigenous potters rapidly took the new form on board.

The invasion of Britain in AD 43, being carefully planned with full logistical support, saw all the army's supplies and equipment replacements, including *mortaria*, initially brought in from Gaul.

In common with other requirements, as the army established itself in Britain, pottery of all types was commissioned locally where possible, and the first *mortaria* were produced in the south at sites such as Brockley Hill, Radlett and *Verulamium* (St. Albans). The name of one immigrant potter at least is known; he came from Gaul to set up his kilns.

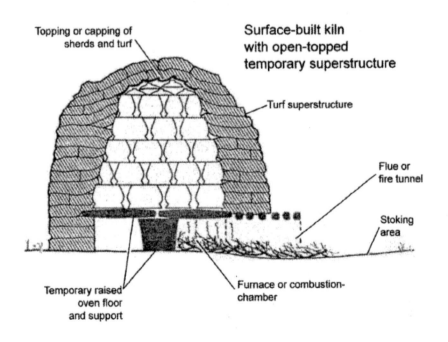

Topping or capping of sherds and turf

Surface-built kiln with open-topped temporary superstructure

Turf superstructure

Flue or fire tunnel

Stoking area

Temporary raised oven floor and support

Furnace or combustion-chamber

The preferred clay for *mortaria* was that which we now refer to as 'pipe-clay'. This is of good quality, fires to a near white fabric, and was also used for small flagons or handled jars with a spout, and lamps. Although a small amount of red-brown ware had been produced in the Mancetter area as early as the mid-first century, it was the discovery of a source of pipe-clay which led to the start-up of the industry towards the end of the century, with potters specialising in the manufacture of *mortaria* quickly moving into this area to set up business. The red-brown ware referred to above may have been supplied to the army occupying the nearby fort, but the army had long gone by the time the *mortaria* production commenced. The popularity of Hartshill/Mancetter ware in the civil market led to an industry of huge proportions with, as noted regarding Sarrius, markets across the Midlands and the North. One must imagine the area as being a Roman Stoke-on-Trent, (reeking with smoke as in the days of the coal-fired bottle ovens), with kilns stretching from the Witherley area to the Hartshill ridge. Over sixty-five kilns have already been recorded and the industry covered many hectares. Kilns were also excavated by Keith Scott at Clock Hill, Hartshill, roughly half way between the main production areas at Mancetter and Hartshill.[14] Undoubtedly there are many more to be found, not to mention those lost and destroyed. As well as the kilns, regard must also be given to workshops, clay storage and transport, water supply, timber for fuel, and not least, accommodation for the many hundreds of workers, and provision for their sustenance.

[14]This sentence was inserted by the editor, Nigel Melton.

48

In addition to several kilns excavated by Kay Hartley at Hartshill, the Broad Close field was completely excavated by her in a series of six-week digs during the 1960s and 1970s. In this field have been found the remains of twenty-three kilns, seven wells, a service road system, a water channelling system from one large well leading across the site, clay puddling pits (when disused these became dumps for wasters), and even a small glass furnace. The whole field was strewn with waster fragments, and nowadays, after ploughing, such material can still be found when field walking. Mrs. Hartley is the country's leading expert on *mortaria*, and her knowledge is of inestimable value to the archaeologist.

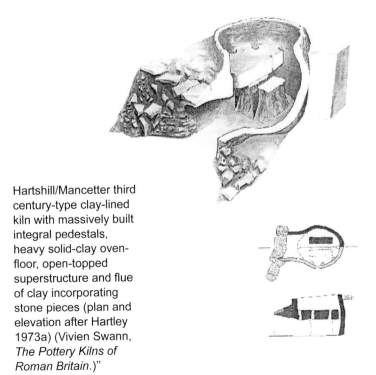

Hartshill/Mancetter third century-type clay-lined kiln with massively built integral pedestals, heavy solid-clay oven-floor, open-topped superstructure and flue of clay incorporating stone pieces (plan and elevation after Hartley 1973a) (Vivien Swann, *The Pottery Kilns of Roman Britain*.)"

49

By the mid-fourth century, the Mancetter potters lost their northern market to the North Yorkshire Crambeck potters and later that century came under severe competitive pressure from the Oxford potters. Even so, Mancetter survived. However, towards the end of the fourth century the economy of Roman Britain was affected by the general problems of the Empire. Being capitalistic enterprises, such large scale industries depended on a monetary system and they also needed good communications and a settled peace. When this began to break down in the late fourth and early fifth century' (the last input of coin to Britain came in AD 402) and major problems were created by Saxon incursions affecting the East coast, quantity pottery production rapidly collapsed. Mancetter may have struggled on for some years serving local requirements presumably on a barter basis, but the widespread marketing was at an end.

The field path continues along the hedge bordering the Broad Close leading towards the crossing of the River Anker and the village of Mancetter beyond. This path provides a vantage point from which to consider the position of the Roman fort on the ridge in the middle distance on the far side of the river. The church and the Manor House are instantly identifiable, and the almshouses to the right of the church also show up clearly. This general view reveals what a superb defensive site was selected by the Roman surveyors.

On entering the next field, if one pauses in the corner and looks back towards Witherley Church, one's eye crosses the field in which Keith Scott found a Roman building of substantial construction. His work revealed part of a hypocaust and evidence that the building had been demolished in the late Roman period. Inserted into the site were Saxon burials and, in view of its importance, English Heritage scheduled it. No further work has been carried out. This is the first building of stone construction that has been found in the Mancetter area and its function is uncertain. Possibilities are a bath-house, a house with integral baths, or even a *mansio* (a sort of Roman motel).

Continuing along the footpath and descending to the river, on the left before the footbridge was a Roman rectangular feature of moderate size. The Mancetter area is very unrewarding for the aerial photographer seeking crop marks, but this feature was noticed by Jim Pickering on one of his many flights and he produced the excellent photograph reproduced on page 17. Keith Scott conducted one of his first excavations in Mancetter on this feature, recovering pottery including Samian[15], but what the site and building was used for is unknown.

[15]The presence of Samian ware demonstrated that the feature was contemporary with the early fortress. (Ed. Nigel Melton)

The crossing of the River Anker heads directly for the East Gate of the fortress, and it is likely that there was a ford, if not a bridge, in roughly the same position as the footbridge. Just beyond lies a mill leat, and the mill itself on the right is 18th/19th century. The supports for the mill wheel are clearly visible from the bridge over the leat, and a mill has been in this position for many centuries.

CHAPTER 5 -
THE BOUDICAN REVOLT

The literary sources available to us relating to the uprising are the works of Tacitus and Cassius Dio. Tacitus, who was also the son-in-law of Agricola, a later Governor of Britain, gives a description of the events in his Annals of Imperial Rome, written in the early years of the second century AD. As well as having access to government records, he probably also drew on Agricola's memories of his service in Britain. A shorter account appears in his biography of Agricola. The other ancient writer describing the period is Cassius Dio in his History of the Roman World. He was writing during the first quarter of the third century AD and may well have drawn upon the works of Tacitus, but he does provide some additional information.

Although there were other earlier underlying causes, the immediate trigger for the uprising was the death of Prasutagus, king of the *Iceni*, an East Anglian tribe inhabiting the area of today's Norfolk and Suffolk. To their south were the *Trinovantes* in today's Essex. Prior to the Roman invasion, this tribe had been conquered, circa AD10, by their western neighbours, the *Catuvellauni*, and the capital of the amalgamated tribes was established at *Camulodunum* (Colchester). The *Iceni* were in a treaty relationship with Rome after the invasion, with the status of client kingdom. Imperial policy towards client kingdoms was governed by their usefulness to Rome.

They often protected a border as buffer states and did not require a garrison, but Rome, when it suited the Empire's interests, would abrogate a treaty using any pretext. The death of the pro-Roman Prasutagus gave the Emperor Nero such a pretext to incorporate the Icenian kingdom into the province of *Britannia*.

The financial administrator of the province, the procurator, Catus Decianus, with his staff and backed by army units, descended on the tribal capital to make an inventory, but things rapidly became nasty. Plundering, as if the kingdom were a prize of war (to quote Tacitus), became endemic; the royal estates and those of the aristocracy were confiscated. Protest by the widow of Prasutagus, Queen Boudica, was disregarded; indeed she was flogged and her two daughters raped. All this was not to be borne and the tribe rose in revolt, bringing with them the *Trinovantes*. The latter had previously been outraged by substantial land seizures in and around *Camulodunum* for the foundation of a *colonia*, a settlement for newly retired legionaries. This was a purpose-built town. However, the barracks and other buildings of the now empty fortress of *Legio XX*, which had been moved to Gloucester, were converted into housing. The defensive ditches and rampart would have been levelled, of course. By AD 60 the *colonia* even had a theatre. In addition a magnificent temple dedicated to Claudius was under construction at this date, having been commenced soon after the death of Claudius in AD 54. This was very much a symbol of Rome's authority, and the *Trinovantes* took the opportunity offered by the great revolt to settle old scores.

54

The governor of *Britannia*, Gaius Suetonius Paulinus, was appointed in AD 58 following the sudden death of his predecessor, Quintus Veranius. The latter had only been in office for twelve months. Paulinus had been briefed to press ahead with the conquest of Wales commenced by Veranius. By the spring of AD 60, starting the campaigning season, he opened up with an attack on the island of Anglesey. This was the Celtic *Mona*, the 'breadbasket' of the North Welsh tribes, and the major druidic centre of Iron-Age Britain. Tacitus gives a graphic account of the attack across the Menai Straits and the subjugation of the island. The Straits are difficult to cross by water, and, notably, Tacitus records the use of flat-bottomed boats to get the infantry across. The term 'landing craft' springs to mind. He also tells us that the cavalry either crossed by fording with riders up, or, in deeper water, the riders swam with their horses. At this juncture, the alarming news of the revolt reached Paulinus.

For the Welsh campaign Paulinus had two legions, the *Legio XIV Gemina* and the greater part of *Legio XX*, together with regiments of auxiliaries both infantry and cavalry. With the legions at full battle strength, the army taking part in the North Wales offensive would have numbered some twenty thousand men. Land routes for access to the Menai Straits opposite *Mona*, namely the Bangor area, would have been along the coast, and, if cleared in previous campaigns, the Vale of Clwyd. By crossing the River Dee at Farndon near the later Roman brick, tile and pottery manufacturing complex at Holt, then via the modern Ruthin area, this crossing would also provide another approach to the left bank of the Dee estuary. Another route which has been suggested follows the general line of the modern A5 up to Betws-y-Coed, thence towards Bangor or the Conway estuary. It is questionable whether this difficult mountainous area had been cleared of the opposing tribes by the date of the new campaign, and was safe to use.

In addition Paulinus would have used the navy for troop and supply transport along the coast; indeed, combined operations were far from unknown in Roman army campaigns!

Research carried out by the Severn Tidal Research Group has revealed that on the Western coasts of Britain the first century AD sea levels, related to today's Mean Sea Level, were some five feet (1.5 metres) higher. At this period, the Dee estuary was typically estuarial with mud flats and sand banks exposed at low tide. Roman shipping, including warships, would have been perfectly able to load at Chester[16]. This harbour area, now dry land, is today known as the Roodee. The estuary continued to be used in later centuries by shipping until silting problems created so much difficulty that the river was canalised from Chester as far as Connah's Quay in the early nineteenth century. By then much of the shipping trade had gone to the developing Liverpool.

[16]I am grateful to Gordon McDonald, Chairman of the S.T.R. Group for the information enabling me to make this observation.

Map 7

THE DEE ESTUARY

Circa AD 50.

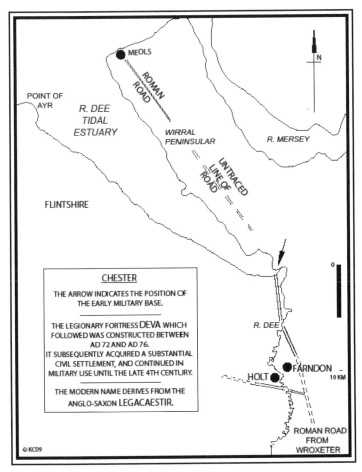

MEOLS

ROMAN ROAD

N

POINT OF AYR

R. DEE TIDAL ESTUARY

WIRRAL PENINSULAR

R. MERSEY

UNTRACED LINE OF ROAD

FLINTSHIRE

CHESTER

THE ARROW INDICATES THE POSITION OF THE EARLY MILITARY BASE.

THE LEGIONARY FORTRESS DEVA WHICH FOLLOWED WAS CONSTRUCTED BETWEEN AD 72 AND AD 76.
IT SUBSEQUENTLY ACQUIRED A SUBSTANTIAL CIVIL SETTLEMENT, AND CONTINUED IN MILITARY USE UNTIL THE LATE 4TH CENTURY.

THE MODERN NAME DERIVES FROM THE ANGLO-SAXON LEGACAESTIR.

R. DEE

FARNDON

HOLT

0

10 KM

ROMAN ROAD FROM WROXETER

© KC09

THIS DEPICTION OF THE TIDAL ESTUARY OF THE RIVER DEE IS BASED ON THE MAP OF A SURVEY CARRIED OUT BY JOHN MACKAY IN 1732, RIVER MAIN COURSE OMITTED.

One further recent discovery concerns the Wirral Peninsula itself. From site finds and investigations at Dove Point, Meols, at the tip, there is firm evidence of a lost port in use throughout the Iron Age, the Roman period, and the Dark Ages.

Third century BC Carthaginian coins have even been found indicating distant trading contacts. There is a partially traced undated Roman road along the spine of the peninsular leading from the Chester area to its tip. How early it was built is uncertain, but it may well have followed an existing much older route.

Chester, the site of a later legionary fortress, has provided evidence of a military presence dating to the fifties AD and it may be presumed to have had port facilities of some sort. The fortress mentioned above replacing that at Wroxeter, circa AD 76-79, was called *Deva*. An extensive extramural civil settlement subsequently developed.

THE SITE OF THE BATTLEFIELD

Ancient battle sites are far from easy to recognise. After the engagement all reusable weapons etc. were recovered, as was any other metal for reworking. The dead were buried in grave pits, or in the case of the Romans, cremated, and after nearly two thousand years no surface evidence can possibly remain. It is just possible that some major excavation, for whatever reason, may hit a burial pit with large quantities of bones or traces thereof. Mancetter is just one possibility. Another site for consideration is the Dunsmore Plain lying to the north-east of Rugby, falling gently away southwards with the Watling Street crossing it, roughly south to north. Heavily wooded on the crest and with open country to the front, this would also match Tacitus's description, except that there is no defile there.[17] The Roman army could even have met Boudica further south still, possibly placing the battlefield in the area of the Chilterns, closer to St. Albans. Thus any site is a possibility along or close to the Watling Street, anywhere between Wall, near Lichfield and St. Albans. Other views favour a site away from the Watling Street to the west of London. The following account can only present a reasoned possibility based on what evidence is available.

[17]Personal comment to the author by the late Jack Lucas, director of the Tripontium excavations.

Map 8

THE SUGGESTED BATTLEFIELD

Circa AD 60.

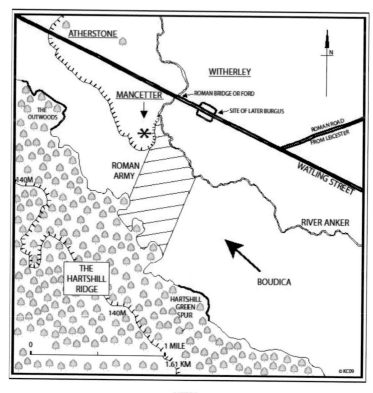

NOTES

1. ✳ - SITE OF FORTRESS DEMOLISHED , CLEARED, AND UNOCCUPIED SINCE CIRCA AD 77.

2. IN INDICATING THE DEPTH OF THE GENERAL POSITION OF THE ROMAN ARMY IT HAS BEEN ASSUMED THAT CAVALRY AND AUXILLIARY REGIMENTS WERE HELD TO THE REAR OF THE LEGIONARIES UNTIL NEEDED. NORMALLY THESE TROOPS WOULD HAVE BEEN ON BOTH FLANKS.

3. MAP BASED ON EARLY MAPPING OF THE ORDNANCE SURVEY.

In order to present a time framework leading up to the final battle, it is now necessary to detail the actions and movements of Boudica's war host and those of the Roman army making its way back from Anglesey. This is essential to permit an assessment of the probable site. All Tacitus tells us is that:

> [Paulinus] chose a position in a defile with a wood behind him. There could be no enemy, he knew, except at his front, where there was open country without cover for ambushes. He drew up his regular troops in close order, with the lighter armed auxiliaries at their flanks, and the cavalry massed on the wings.[18]

Tacitus also states that the British were in unprecedented numbers, and that confident of an easy victory they brought their wives to watch, "installing them in the baggage carts stationed at the edge of the battlefield."[19]

A Roman army on the march during a campaign was carefully organised for efficiency and security; cavalry forming the advance guard, then the infantry, followed by the artillery, baggage, and supply train, which in turn was followed by an infantry and cavalry rearguard. There would also be flank guards. A day's march could

[18]Tacitus *Annals* 14.34 trans. Grant, 1956.
[19]Tacitus, op cit, 14.34

61

be between twelve and twenty-four miles (19 and 39 kilometres). Modern Roman army reconstruction groups have carried out research on the subject and one body of very fit members, over four days in full armour with weapons and packs, achieved twenty-five miles (40 kilometres) per day at a cost of near exhaustion and severe chafing by the finish. At the end of a day's march, a so-called marching camp was constructed with rampart complete with staked breastwork and ditch. This delineated the area of the camp, but was not specially intended for defence. Tent lines were laid out 'according to the book' with the H.Q. together with the commanding officer's accommodation and that of the senior officers (the legate and the tribunes and staff) in the centre area. All this was so organised that everyone knew precisely their place in case of a 'stand–to.' They were also aware of simple but important factors such as where to go for food, water, supplies, latrines, etc. and to facilitate the quick striking of camp the following day.

Paulinus got his army moving, and would have sent gallopers to call in all available troops in the area of his operations, and, of the highest importance, an order to *Legio II* now at Exeter, to march north to join him. He then decided to acquaint himself with the facts, and taking the view that London was very likely to be the next target for the rebels, he made a fast journey to the town, accompanied by cavalry. London, like Colchester, was undefended, but since the invasion in AD 43 had become a bustling commercial centre. Its position on the River Thames was at the best possible lowest bridging point on the river, and consequently it became a communications hub and an entrepôt centre for both coastal and cross-Channel trade. Even though founded so early, it had a rectilinear street grid, a forum (market-place) and a town council. It was also the site of the province's treasury, the procurator's office. There were virtually no stone buildings, all houses, warehouses, and commercial premises being constructed in timber, with wattle and clay daub and/or unfired clay bricks. The latter are not an unusual building material and are of course laid dry. Plastered and painted they make perfectly satisfactory premises. Dampness must be excluded, and the modern equivalent is the 'cob walled' house found in Devon, for example. The population of London comprised immigrant businessmen, craftsmen, merchants, and their families, together with pro-Roman Britons and the usual underclass of workers and slaves. There would also have been government employees, in particular those belonging to the procurator's staff.

Once in London, it quickly became apparent to Paulinus that it was impossible to save the town from the wrath to come and he had no alternative but to abandon it to its fate, returning up the Watling Street to rejoin his army. The people were advised to save themselves, but as a token, those able to travel fast with his cavalry were permitted to accompany him. As to the rest, a place on any vessel capable of crossing the Channel must have been a lifesaving prize – (one is reminded of the last helicopters out of Saigon in recent American history – and one is also inclined to think that the Roman-era boat owners would charge appropriately!). Among the vanguard of those fleeing was the infamous Catus Decianus, whose actions had started it all. Whilst there is no evidence, it also seems probable that many others fled into the countryside south of London, in particular to the tribal area of *Regni* whose ruler was pro-Roman. Centred on Chichester, this was another client kingdom. Those who remained were caught in a holocaust of slaughter – the British took no prisoners – and, as with Colchester, the town was looted and then torched. The so-called destruction horizon of burned daub and ash also reveals itself in archaeological excavations.

News of the revolt and the danger facing Colchester had of course also rapidly reached the legate of *Legio IX Hispana*, stationed at their half legionary fortress at Longthorpe, near Peterborough. The legate, Petillius Cerialis, set off with part of the legion and cavalry to relieve the town. His force was ambushed and the infantry destroyed. Cerialis himself barely escaped with his life, and fled back to the Longthorpe fortress with his surviving cavalry. There the *Legio IX* remained holed up and impotent until the rebellion was quashed.

Boudica and her military council of tribal chieftains would have been well aware of the Roman army marching south-east to engage the rebels, and realised that, if Paulinus were defeated, the hand of Rome would be lifted from Britain. After all their successes so far during the revolt, it was clear that they confidently expected this could be achieved. The British war host, having destroyed London, then set out up the Watling Street in order to bring the Roman army to battle. En-route, the small Romanised town of *Verulamium* (St. Albans), was also looted and torched. Here, however, it seems possible that the population had time to flee. Tacitus records that Roman and provincial deaths in and near the three towns destroyed by the Boudican forces were an estimated seventy thousand. The big problem for the modern archaeologist is: where is the evidence? Even taking into account the post-holocaust clearance of the towns and the rebuilding, no victims associated with the undisturbed destruction horizon have been discovered, except one disarticulated and charred skeleton in Colchester. Clearance must have been extremely thorough.

On the Roman side, Paulinus had to disengage his troops from Anglesey, get them back to the Dee estuary, then Wroxeter and onwards down the Watling Street. Accompanied by his cavalry unit, he managed to get to London before the British. He appraised the situation and returned to his army which was already on the march. Paulinus had to collect all troops available, and expected the *Legio II*, at least in part, to join him. Even under pressure it is doubtful that the army could have maintained a maximum marching speed and it seems likely that he would not have wished to exhaust his men or leave baggage and supplies behind to catch up.

Another factor to be considered is the route that Paulinus ordered the dispersed units to use. There was the military road up the Severn Valley from Gloucester to Wroxeter and thence northwards via Whitchurch. The main cross country route from the south-west was the Fosse Way heading for Leicester and beyond into Lincolnshire, which crossed the Watling Street at High Cross. This was the communications link associated with the early Fosse *limes*[20], but still very much in use. A further route struck off the Fosse Way near Bourton-on-the-Water heading for Wall on the Watling Street and beyond for Littlechester, Derby. The course of the road known as the Ryknield Street may be seen in Sutton Park where the *agger*, the raised embankment, is clearly visible. In Birmingham itself, the Ryknield Street is joined by another road coming up from the lower Severn Valley via Worcester and Droitwich.

On rejoining the army, Paulinus must have been surprised, and seriously concerned, to find that no troops from the *Legio II* had arrived to reinforce his numbers. As it later emerged, the acting commander of the legion at Exeter, the camp prefect, Poenius Postumus, disobeyed orders and failed to move. What is unknown is the whereabouts of the legate and the senior tribune, (second in command). Were they absent conducting military operations in the south-west, leaving only a token force available to Postumus? Was the countryside alive with 'British freedom fighters', making it

[20]*Limes* – The fortified boundary of the Roman Empire.

impossible to march north without losing control of the entire South-West? One can only speculate, but after the final battle Postumus committed suicide, falling on his sword, because he had cheated *Legio II* of their share of the victory by disobeying the orders of his commander-in-chief, Paulinus.

If the identification of Mancetter as the battle site is correct, it is possible to speculate that Paulinus's last field camp, (or even his main assembly point) before the engagement was at Wall near Lichfield, Staffordshire, where there was military activity of this period; but there is nothing definite to confirm such a possibility. The vicinity of Wall on the western side does offer a very suitable position for a large marching camp. Returning to the description of the battle given to us by Tacitus, we are looking for "a defile" with woods to the rear. Undoubtedly Paulinus, a very experienced general, would have carefully selected the battlefield to make the best possible use of his forces, which were out-numbered by the enemy, and a defile position preventing outflanking and progressively cramping the Boudican attack makes good sense.

An important factor to be considered is the Roman army's line of battle. Normally at this period, the legionaries would be grouped in three ranks, those in the rear ranks moving into the front as required to fill gaps created by wounds or death. A fully equipped legionary soldier had, as weaponry, two javelins (*pilae*) a short stabbing sword (*gladius*) and a dagger (*pugio*), and the large rectangular shield (*scutum*). This was made of plywood with a metal boss, and the edge trimmed in bronze strip. (Fragments of the latter are often found during excavations). The shield was slightly curved and protected the body from neck to knee. It was painted, and emblazoned with the emblem of Jupiter's thunderbolt. Each soldier occupied the space of three feet (91 cms) in the battle line. This spacing is the critical factor since one legion in its battle formation occupied a frontage of approximately one mile (1.6 kilometres), at full fighting strength. In addition there were auxiliary units accompanying the legions. The *Legio XX* was not present in full strength, as Tacitus records, but if the heavily armed and armoured regular troops numbered say eight to nine thousand, space must still be found for the auxiliary, infantry and cavalry and possibly archers on either flank. Tacitus states that Paulinus had only "ten thousand armed men" but modern scholarship considers that this figure is a substantial understatement, deliberately intended to show the Roman army in an even better light to his literary public! Dr. Graham Webster's view is that Paulinus had approaching twenty thousand troops.

All this influences the consideration of the site of the battlefield. Dr. Webster, taking all factors into account, favoured the Mancetter area, with the "defile" into the Hartshill ridge lying to the west of the Watling Street. There is a problem, however, in fitting the Roman battle array into this topography, further complicated by the River Anker which lies between the ridge and the Watling Street.

Paulinus had to ensure that his army was not outflanked and it is most unlikely he would have left the Watling Street river crossing unguarded. Good military strategy would suggest that he placed flanking troops on the higher ground on the left bank of the River Anker with the bridge destroyed. On this higher ground now stands Mancetter church and the Manor, the site of the vacated and demolished half legionary fortress (grid ref. SP 320 967) of *Legio XIV Gemina* before it moved to Wroxeter in the second half of the AD fifties.

From the Hartshill ridge looking across the Leicestershire plain towards Charnwood Forest in Leicestershire.

It seems probable that this left flank would have been held by auxiliary troops. Between this higher ground and the Hartshill ridge lies a valley which runs northwest, skirting modern Atherstone, and through it runs the present railway and canal. Atherstone itself lies on the line of the Watling Street. Paulinus's main body of troops would be placed across this valley and the battle line would then extend as far as the Hartshill Green spur on the ridge. This suggested disposition moves the scene of action well away from the course of the River Anker and offers the possibility of a fighting retreat if the battle were lost.

THE BATTLE

Having chosen his battleground and knowing full well that Boudica was as anxious to fight as he was himself, Paulinus would have ensured his men were fed and rested beforehand, this being normal Roman army procedure before a major engagement. The troops, with the enemy approaching (scouts would undoubtedly have reported) would then have been grouped up as described by Tacitus. An effort of imagination is required, but one must picture the silent ranks of the legionaries flanked by the auxiliaries, and contrast this with the vast numbers of the Boudican war host preparing themselves for the attack. Tacitus tells us that their warrior Queen drove around all the tribes to urge them on to victory "They will never face the din and roar of our thousands, much less the shock of our onslaught" he states, putting a speech into her mouth[21]. Paulinus also makes a speech to his army, similarly to encourage the men. It was standard literary convention for such pre-battle speeches to be included in their accounts by the ancient authors. (Perhaps the sentiments expressed by the general to his senior commanders in the pre-battle councils were remembered and worked up into resounding phraseology!)

---

[21]Tacitus *Annals* 14.35 trans. Grant 1956

At last the British formed up their ranks and charged. As soon as the hordes were within range, the legionaries launched two volleys of their javelins (*pilae*). The effect on the oncoming British was catastrophic. The *pilum* when it struck, even if it failed to kill or wound, would render a shield useless. Some twenty thousand such missiles hitting unarmoured men in the space of a few minutes would bring the charge to a state of chaos. This was the moment of opportunity for the legionary soldiers to draw their relatively short stabbing swords, and burst forward on the opposing disorganised enemy. The Celtic weaponry consisted of the slashing sword, the spear, and for defence, a round/oval shield; as mentioned above, body armour was not worn. A slashing sword implies room to swing or raise, and facing an armoured, shielded opponent, the tribesman leaves his body unprotected, and the result is a sword thrust in his torso. The crowding of the masses of the British warriors completely inhibited their style of combat against the well-disciplined legionaries, and inevitably they were slaughtered by the thousand. By now the Roman auxiliaries would have joined the attack adding to the legions' weight.

In due course, the British began to break and flee; but as will be recalled, they had lined up carts on the edge of the battlefield to permit their women folk to watch the fray, and this line of wagons created a barrier to escape. In addition, the auxiliary cavalry now came into action to chase and kill and prevent any defensive grouping of the enemy. Paulinus's men had the British trapped and the battle now turned into a massacre. In the Roman frenzy even the women and the baggage animals were killed. For Rome it was "a glorious victory"; for Boudica and the *Iceni* and *Trinovantes* it was a disaster of the first magnitude, and the start of a nightmarish sequence of events in the tribal home territories.

Tacitus tells us[22] that "our own casualties were about four hundred dead, and a slightly larger number of wounded". He also says "according to one report almost eighty thousand Britons fell". This figure sounds considerably exaggerated, but undoubtedly the British casualties were very great. Once the fighting ceased, captives may very well have been taken – who better to clear up the site and dig burial pits? The legions looked after their own of course, and their dead were cremated. Tacitus also reports that Boudica poisoned herself, but it is unknown if her suicide occurred away from the scene of her defeat. Her failure and death was the last major attempt by Celtic Britain to free the country from Roman rule.

[22]Tacitus *Annals* 14.37. trans. Grant 1956

THE AFTERMATH

Suetonius Paulinus and his victorious army now returned to the lowland areas of the Midlands and the South-East to re-pacify the province, put down any further show of resistance, and to extract revenge for the atrocities committed by the *Iceni* and *Trinovantes* during the uprising. Old fort sites were reoccupied and rebuilt, Mancetter and The Lunt at Baginton being two local examples. New strategic forts were established, and Tacitus records that Paulinus kept the army "under canvas to finish the war"[23] – strictly speaking the translation should be 'under leather', since the army's tents were made up of sections of hide.[24] The half legionary fortress site at Mancetter has revealed the details of the second smaller fort – undoubtedly for an auxiliary unit. Reinforcements had to be provided from the Continent to replace losses. Two thousand legionaries were needed, mainly to bring the *Legio IX Hispana* up to strength. Eight auxiliary infantry cohorts amounting to four thousand men, and two cavalry units (*alae)*, totalling one thousand men and their mounts, were also sent.

[23]Tacitus *Annals* 14.38. trans. Grant 1956

[24]A section from a leather tent was recovered from the waterlogged fill of a well in the Mill Lane excavation.

The implication of Tacitus' statement is that the army spent months in the field over the winter of AD 60-61. The tribal homelands of the *Iceni* and the *Trinovantes* were "ravaged with fire and the sword", and still the "British tribesmen were disinclined for peace". To quote Leonard Cottrell's felicitous phrases in his book *The Great Invasion*: "The familiar, hopeless pattern was beginning again; hate breeding hate; oppression breeding revolt; atrocity by the repressed, answered by atrocity by the oppressor". To make matters worse, with all the available manpower caught up in Boudica's war host, the crops had not been sown, so with no harvest brought in, famine also struck. The British had expected to capture the Roman army's stocks of supplies, of which grain was pre-eminent.

With pacification in hand, a new imperial procurator was appointed by the emperor as successor to the vanished Catus Decianus (what became of him is unrecorded.). The procurator, the financial agent of a province, reported directly to the emperor and was not a subordinate of the governor – an early example of checks and balances! This turned out to be an important factor as will be seen.

The immediate task on arrival of the new procurator, Caius Julius Alpinus Classicianus, was to re-establish his department and to regain financial control. Previously based in London, which had been destroyed in the uprising, he may have had to install himself somewhere south of the River Thames in an unaffected area.

Alternatively, bearing in mind the communications hub represented by London, a rapid rebuild of suitable premises and accommodation for the staff may have been put in hand.

It became clear to Classicianus within a relatively short time that if Paulinus persisted in his ferocious retribution policy, the province would be ruined. Apart from the loss of life and resentment to Roman rule created among even the more peaceful peoples, there was the pragmatic view that the tax base of the province was in the course of being destroyed. Classicianus reported his findings to the Emperor Nero, recommending that Paulinus be replaced and a conciliatory regime be introduced. Obviously this report faced Nero with a major problem, namely how could he withdraw a governor who had recently won a great victory and held *Britannia* for Rome.

A top civil servant of the imperial secretariat named Polyclitus was despatched to Britain in order to make an independent assessment, and later in the year (AD 61) some months after receipt of his report, Nero grasped the nettle and, seizing on a minor incident when a few ships were lost (the circumstances are unrecorded), Paulinus was withdrawn. However, he did not lose favour, and continued in a political career in Rome thereafter.

The new governor, Petilius Turpilianus, and his successor spent the next ten years in reconciliation and rebuilding both confidence and the destroyed towns. Priority was given to Colchester, which being a symbol of Rome's power, warranted immediate action. (A *colonia* was in effect an extension of the city of Rome itself within a province). The destruction debris shows little or no evidence of weathering, indicating a swift commencement of the work, and undoubtedly the "Temple of the Deified Claudius" would have been given the utmost priority. The rebuilt *colonia* was settled by discharged legionary veterans once again, and there is an inscription which refers to a new name for the old *Camulodunum: Colonia Victricensis*. (It is possible, however, that the 'City of Victory' name may have even been given at the time of the founding of the first *colonia*.)

Other public buildings would have been tackled, but additionally the town was now provided with a defensive wall. Colchester was the first town in Britain to have this and it would be many years before stone was used again in town defences. It was a major engineering work and would have taken several years to complete. In addition to the wall circuit, approaching two miles (3.20 kilometres) in length, there were six gates, and at least twelve interval towers. For the modern visitor there are still long stretches of the wall to be seen. All this cost a great deal, and there must have been central government finance made available – perhaps this is not surprising since Colchester had been, and still was, the capital of Roman Britain.

The rebuilding of London, and its re-establishment as a port and business centre was rather slower. The procurator's department, if not there during AD 61, would return as soon as possible, providing a big boost to the town. Excavations show, however, that in large areas a gap of ten years existed before even clearance was commenced, let alone new building. This said, it was far from deserted, although it took time for the merchants and businessmen and craftsmen to return to Britain to start up again. What is clear from post-World War Two excavations, is that in the AD seventies a massive building programme began. Stone buildings were erected, including a forum with associated offices and bath houses. Near Cannon Street was a palace-like building which the excavator suggested was for the governor. As with Colchester it would seem that all this was funded by central government. The possible palace implies that the seat of government of the province had been transferred to London from Colchester, making it the new capital of Roman Britain. An explanation for the decision may lie not only in London's hub position in the road network, but in the ability of the River Thames to furnish deep-water harbour facilities for ocean-going ships directly alongside the town. Very substantial port facilities were included in the rebuilding programmes.

St. Albans, small to begin with, lay derelict and deserted. It was not until the governorship of Julius Agricola, which commenced in AD 77, that it was re-founded. Fragments of an inscription confirms the completion of the construction of the forum complex in AD 79 under his governorship.

The two legions directly involved in the victory over Boudica were awarded battle honours by the Emperor. *Legio XIV Gemina* was granted the additional title of *Martia Victrix*, and the *Legio XX* likewise received the honorific *Valeria Victrix*.

EPILOGUE

It is rarely possible to make a direct connection between the inscription on a tomb monument and a known personage (emperors and the like excepted), even someone who had a major influence on the history of Roman Britain. With Julius Classicianus, the post-Boudican Chief Financial Officer, appointed Procurator in AD 61, we are extremely fortunate.

During what was a period of barbarian scares, sea-borne raids across the North Sea, and invasions across the Rhine frontier, the later Roman Empire in the West undertook wide-spread defensive construction to improve the security of towns still lacking walls. A ready source of large worked stone was available from the tomb monuments located in the towns' earlier cemeteries. Generally the blocks were used in the foundations of walls and bastions, providing a substantial base for their construction. Neumagen in the Mosel Valley, Germany, is the outstanding example of this. In London, two excavations in the vicinity of the Tower of London, which took place in 1852 and again in 1935, recovered a number of large blocks from the tomb monument of Julius Classicianus which had been used in the foundations of a bastion of the city wall.

Of the inscription, enough appears on the recovered stones to permit a reconstruction of the text, clearly identifying the man and his position. There are six lines of lettering, but unfortunately the line or lines covering the earlier career of Classicianus are missing and undoubtedly remain to be discovered below ground not far away. Such an important find, showing that Classicianus died during his posting to *Britannia* and was cremated in London, is fascinating in itself, but there is another twist to the story. The tombstone was set up by his wife, the appropriate two lines of text being as follows:

IVLIA .INDI.FILIA.PACATA.INDIANA
VXOR

This tells us that Julia Pacata (**IVLIA....PACATA.**) was the daughter of Indus (**INDI. FILIA**), something of which she must have been very proud, to include it on the memorial to her husband. Her father was Julius Indus, a Romanised Gaul, an aristocrat of the *Treveri*, inhabiting the region of modern Trier and the Mosel Valley. He is recorded by Tacitus as having assisted in the quelling of a rebellious movement among the *Treveri* during the reign of the Emperor Tiberius. Earlier he had founded a Gallic cavalry regiment from among his tribal countrymen, named the

"Ala Indiana"; this was among some twenty similar troops of Gallic cavalry established about the same time bearing the name of their founder, and becoming 'instant' regiments of auxiliaries for the Roman army. The *Ala Indiana* originally saw service on the Rhine, and subsequently formed part of the AD 43 invasion task force. A cavalryman of Indus' Horse, one Dannicus, died in Cirencester after sixteen years service. His tombstone is in the Corinium Museum.

Classicianus himself came from a Gallic family which had been awarded Roman citizenship, probably under Augustus, taking additional Roman names, and clearly he had entered and made his career in the Imperial civil service. His reconstructed tombstone may be seen at the British Museum.

CHAPTER 6
- THE ROMAN ARMY

THE LEGIONS

The main fighting force of the Roman Army was the Legion, composed of heavily armed and armoured infantry, totalling approximately five thousand men, divided into basic units called 'centuries', of eighty men each.

Each legionary was equipped, as his body armour, with a flexible cuirass with shoulder protection. It was made of a series of iron plates and extremely well designed for its purpose. The cuirass was called the *lorica segmentata* (*lorica* for short), and for head protection, the soldier had a helmet with neck guard and hinged side pieces to protect the face. His shield was called the *scutum*. It was large, rectangular, and slightly curved around the front of his body, protecting it from neck to knee. The shield was painted and emblazoned with the emblem of Jupiter's

Roman soldier (*courtesy of Lunt Fort*)

thunderbolt. Construction was of plywood with a metal boss and the edges were trimmed with bronze strips. When not in use in battle or on formal parade it had a fabric cover.

As to weaponry, the legionary carried a stabbing sword, the *gladius*, which was sheathed on the right hand side of the body; a dagger, the *pugio*, but additionally two throwing spears, or javelins, the *pilum*, (plural *pilae*).

The legion was made up of ten 'cohorts', nine of which comprised six centuries. Each cohort totalled 480 men. The first cohort was, however, of five double centuries, totalling 800 men in all.

Hence, with each century of 80 men we have the following:-

One century:	80 legionaries		
One cohort:	480 legionaries x 9	=	4,320
1st cohort:	160 legionaries x 5	=	800
			5,120

Each century was officered by a 'centurion' and to the total of these centurions must be added the senior centurion, the *primus pilus*, the 'first spear'   60

5,180

In addition to the infantry, there was a detachment of horse acting as escorts, messengers, and despatch riders; on campaign they would additionally be used as scouts: 120

Thus, fully manned the fighting strength is: 5,300

THE OFFICERS

LEGATUS LEGIONIS

The commanding officer, the 'legate', was of the senatorial class of Roman society. After several years in this appointment, which was made by the Emperor, he would return to the civil side of his career. Clearly, he would have had military experience and ability, and, in command of a legion, he had a substantial staff, not only at headquarters, but also personal.

TRIBUNUS LATICLAVUS

Tribuna laticlava were up-and-coming young men of the equestrian class (the much later mediaeval equivalent would be knights). Again, these 'tribunes', of which there were six, were on short-term employment to the army as a career step. The senior tribune, who was second in command of the legion, was serving prior to entering the Senate.

PRAEFECTUS CASTORUM

The camp prefect was responsible for the upkeep of the legionary fortress, its equipment, and supplies. He was also of the equestrian class, but had a much longer period of service in the army. The camp prefect was third in command of the legion.

THE *PRIMUS PILUS* and the CENTURIONS
It is difficult to rank these men, who were vital for the proper functioning of the legion. It would perhaps be correct to class them as very senior N.C.O.s in modern day parlance – just a speculative thought.

THE LEGIONARY FORTRESS

The home of the legion at this mid-first century period, was of timber construction with a turf and timber rampart, and had an area of approximately fifty acres (20 hectares).

Every eighty-man century occupied one barrack building comprising ten accommodation rooms, each with a second room for equipment storage. The centurion had separate quarters at one end of the building. On campaign, the eight-man units shared one tent. The centurion had his own, adjacent. The eight-man unit was called a *contubernium*.

The fortress housed all the headquarters' staff, including clerical and other non-combatants, in a substantial building centrally situated known as the *principia*. This had a range of offices and store-rooms in colonnades surrounding a gravelled or paved central area. Fronting this lay an enormous cross-hall of basilican plan, stretching the whole width of the *principia*. The main entrance to the building was centrally placed here. On the far side of the paved area opposite were further offices, and again centrally placed was the shrine, the *sacellum*, where the legion's standards were kept; beneath this lay secure housing for the legionary pay chest and bank.

The legate's residence, next to the *principia*, was also a substantial building (almost the size of a small-palace), known as the *praetorium*. It also accommodated all the legate's personal and slave staff. The houses of the military tribunes lay nearby.

Other buildings within the fortress included granaries (a year's supply of grain was held!), workshops, stabling, latrines and provision for cooking and baking. Normally situated outside the fortress wall, because of the possible fire risk, lay the bathhouse, which in addition to its obvious functions provided a sort of social centre for the troops. Even at this early period it was largely constructed of brick and stone. Not to be overlooked is the extramural civil settlement which rapidly developed after the fort's occupation by the legion, providing for the soldier's other needs and social amenities.

THE AUXILIA

Auxiliary regiments, with their specialities, complemented the legion's heavy infantry. At this period - the Early Empire - only a Roman citizen could join a legion, but the auxiliaries were drawn from non-Roman allied and newly conquered nations. On completion of his service, twenty-five years, the discharged veteran was granted Roman citizenship. He also received a formal discharge certificate. This was engraved on two bronze plates, approximately six inches (15 cms) square, and listed his career. Occasionally fragments of these turn up on excavations and provide much very useful information. Very rarely is a complete one found.

THREE TYPES OF AUXILIARY UNIT

There were three types of auxiliary unit, as follows:

ALA.

> Composed of cavalry, nominal strength five hundred, divided into sixteen troops of horse with thirty two riders per troop. A small number of *alae* were of one thousand men. Clearly an *ala* must have had other non-riders in the unit. A troop commander was called a *decurio* and his troop a *turma*.
>
> The *ala* Commander was called a *praefectus*, and was a Roman citizen of the equestrian class. Particularly with the larger *alae*, it was quite a prestigious post.

COHORS PEDITATA.

As the name implies, this was composed of infantry. As with the legions, it was divided into eighty-man centuries, each officered by a centurion. The cohort commander was called a *praefectus cohortis*. There were, of course, other officers and Headquarters staff; and as with the *Ala* regiments, some of the infantry regiments were double size, of one thousand men.

COHORS EQUITATA.

A unit combining cavalry and infantry, normally of a strength of five hundred, but again some of one thousand. A quarter of the manpower was mounted. In the 'pecking order' of the auxiliaries these mixed units were of the lowest grade, and the troops were not of the highest standard and training. It is considered they were used for patrolling, reconnaissance, escort duties, and as messengers. Notwithstanding, they were also used in warfare as skirmishers. The commander was also called a *praefectus cohortis*.

AUXILIARY UNIT EQUIPMENT.

Infantry were armed with sword and an oval shield, and there were spearmen, archers, sling-men, etc. Body armour normally consisted of chain mail, but there is slight evidence that some units had similar armour to legionaries. Cavalry obviously carried lances as well as swords and shields, and wore chain mail. The auxiliary regiments presented a very mixed picture, but all their specialities were invaluable to the Roman army.

AUXILIARY UNIT FORTS.

The permanent base for auxiliaries was the fort of similar construction to, but very much smaller than, the legionary fortress. The area and accommodation depended on the type of unit and size; between four and ten acres (1.5 and 4 hectares) is the average.

APPENDIX 1 - THE ARRANGEMENTS OF A FORT'S DEFENSIVE SYSTEM

As mentioned in Chapter 2, the Mancetter fortress follows a standard pattern of construction for the first century AD; that is, a turf and timber rampart with two ditches and, further out, a punic ditch. There were, of course, always variations according to site, especially as to the number of ditches.

The rampart was built up with material from the excavated ditches contained within an outer skin of carefully laid turf. Trajan's Column in Rome has excellent illustrations of legionaries engaged in fort building, using blocks of turf. A timber framework was erected, contained within the rampart, providing support for the timber parapet and the fighting platform. Access to this parapet walk was provided by steps at regular intervals (this was called an *ascensus*), leading up from the roadway immediately behind the rampart. Gateways were of heavy timber construction, and there were interval towers. The reconstructed rampart, gateway and ditch at The Lunt, Baginton,

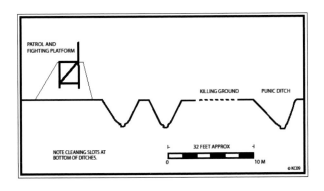

give an accurate impression of these defences and their layout.

The two 'V' shaped ditches in front of the rampart needed regular maintenance (as did the rampart itself), and archaeological excavations regularly reveal a cleaning slot of shovel-width in the bottom.

Some thirty-five feet (11 metres) further out from the inner ditches lay the so-called punic ditch. This is designed to have its outer slope quite steep, with the inner more gentle. Punic is the Semitic language of the Carthaginian nation, long an enemy of Rome. (Carthage may, of course, be seen by today's visitor to Tunisia.) Rome considered the Carthaginians treacherous and deceitful, and in designing this type of ditch, the army applied the adjective 'punic' to it. The intended function is as follows:-

In an enemy attack upon a fort, the oncoming infantry would first cross the punic ditch, scaling the gentle inner slope with ease. Moving rapidly across the stretch of open ground before them, they would reach the first of the two inner ditches. If fire had not already been opened up by the defending garrison, a hail of javelins, arrows and carroballista bolts would now be unleashed. Retreat would have been inevitable and the enemy had to re-cross what had become a veritable 'killing ground'. On reaching the punic ditch and still under fire, the fleeing attackers would leap into it and

90

then be faced with a difficult climb out, with missiles continuing to hit their backs.

Treacherous indeed, as the name implies!

APPENDIX 2 - ROMAN SAMIAN POTTERY

Samian has been mentioned several times in connection with finds during the excavations at Mancetter, and details always appear in the published reports. It would seem worthwhile, therefore, to include a note on the subject and its importance.

This high-quality red-gloss ware was exported from the manufacturing centres in Gaul to many parts of the Roman Empire. For example, an unopened crate was discovered in Pompeii that had just arrived before the eruption of Vesuvius!

In Britain, the ubiquitous name 'Samian' is used to describe the pottery, but on the Continent the term *terra sigillata* tends to be used. This means 'figured ware', but is not really accurate since there was also a huge production of plain ware as well as the decorated ware.

From very early times, the word 'Samian' was used by the Romans to describe any red-slipped ware. They were looking back to Greek origins of red decorated ware, and somewhere along the line associated the name of the island of Samos with this. Greek black decorated ware was also known and admired. (Were they seeking a way of distinguishing the two types? Just a thought.)

Over the centuries the Italian pottery industry developed in techniques, quality, and style and the ancestor of what we call Samian was that centred at Arezzo in Tuscany. This is known as Arretine ware. Following the conquest of Gaul the process of Romanisation commenced, and with it the development of commerce and manufacturing. Certain potters from Arezzo set up in the Lyons area, suitable clay having been discovered there, but it was not long before the right type of clay was also found in the Garonne river basin in southern France. By AD 25, production at this South Gaulish Samian pottery centre was in full swing. There were two main centres, Montans and La Graufesenque; the first kilns were at Montans, but La Graufesenque eclipsed Montans in size and importance fairly quickly. The product was of very high quality, but towards the end of the century this seems to have deteriorated and output was much reduced. Other Samian sites were developed in central and north-eastern Gaul, and it is considered that the production of South Gaulish Samian ceased by AD 110.

An enormous amount of research has been undertaken into Samian pottery and its manufacture since scholarly interest was first aroused in the nineteenth century. Types, forms, decorations, kilns and makers' stamps have all been researched; this continues with added intensity. Even the fabric of a pot with the colour of the clay and possible inclusions can be helpful. The clay used in the production of Samian, and of course the slip coat, contains a micaceous mineral called illite. Prior to firing, this lies flat in the slip coating of the pot, and the iridescence created by the tiny glittering scales produces the rich red gloss in the finished product.

Samian is a high quality ware mainly for table use and it may be compared with present day Doulton, Worcester, Wedgwood and the like. It arrived in Britain with the army and the accompanying administration in AD 43, followed by traders. Its quality and status caused its use to spread quite rapidly into the higher echelons of the indigenous population. From thence it moved downwards and even one decorated bowl could become a treasured family possession. There is nothing new under the sun!

Among the earlier researchers the name of Dragendorf is pre-eminent; he it was who developed a system of numerical classification of Samian forms. His system continues in use, together with several subsidiary systems added subsequently. A particular type of a decorated South Gaulish bowl is a DR. (Dragendorf) Form 29. A fine example of such a bowl was recovered at Mancetter. Although it was broken, the sherds were large and when re-assembled was eighty percent complete. The base bore the stamp of the potter Murranus who worked at

A large section of a Samian pottery bowl decorated with the scene of a bear hunt, found close to Quarry Lane, Mancetter.

Montans. Interestingly, this was not his normal style of decoration and it seems to have been made from a 'bought-in' mould, most unusual for this potter; indeed the 'bear hunt' decoration in the lower zone is not normally found on South Gaulish ware, and freestyle decoration is also unusual. The bowl is considered to be dated AD 45-55.

All the Mancetter fortress Samian is dated to the mid-first century South Gaulish period, and the greater part was from La Graufesenque. This alone permits the secure dating of the occupation of the fortress site, and is an indication of the value of this pottery as a dating tool.

APPENDIX 3 - THE BASIC ROMAN CURRENCY SYSTEM, FROM AUGUSTUS TO DIOCLETIAN

GOLD		SILVER		BRASS		BRASS		COPPER
Aureus		Denarius		Sestertius		Dupondius		As
1	=	25	=	100	=	200	=	400
		1	=	4	=	8	=	16
				1	=	2	=	4
						1	=	2

The above list does not include smaller denominations.

In A.D. 214 Caracalla introduced a new silver coin, a double denarius. It is uncertain what it was called, but it is referred to as an *antoninianus*.

The next coinage reform was under Diocletian (AD 284 - 305), with further major reforms under Constantine the Great (A.D. 307 - 337), when the gold solidus was introduced, and there were other substantial changes.

APPENDIX 4 –
ARCHAEOLOGICAL
EXCAVATIONS DIRECTED BY
KEITH SCOTT 1964 – 1999

(Prepared by the late Nick Woolridge, and Nigel Melton)

Abbreviations:

B.W.A.S   *Transactions of the Birmingham & Warwickshire Archaeological Society*

W.M.A.N.S.   *West Midlands Archaeological News Sheet (Council for British Archaeology [C.B.A.], Group 8)*

W.M.A.   *West Midlands Archaeology, C.B.A. Group 8.*

ROMAN SITES

1964   Tile Kiln in Arbury Estate, Chilvers Coton

1968   Tile Kiln at Griff Hill Farm

              Scott,K., 'Two Romano-British Tile Kilns',
              B.W.A.S.,Vol. 84, pages 7-17.

1968   Mancetter Fort, East Defences, Almshouse
              Ditch

              Scott, K, 'Two Romano-British Tile Kilns,'
              B.W.A.S., Vol 85, Scott, pages 211-213

1971   Romano-British Tile Kilns in Arbury Estate

              Scott, K, 'Roman-British Tile Kilns: the Arbury

Tilery (continued),' B.W.A.S., Vol.87, pages 57-67.

1975	Scott ,K, 'Watling Street: the River Anker crossing,' W.M.A.S. Vol. 18, pages 51-52
1976-1977	Mancetter Fort, Site 1, the Manor Farmhouse garden
1977	Mancetter Fort, Site 2, Quarry Lane
1977	Mancetter Fort, Site 4, cropmark by the river
1979	Mancetter Fort, Site 3, the West Defences
	Sites 1-4 above, Scott, K. 'Mancetter Village: a first century fort,' B.W.A.S., Vol. 91, *Transactions for 1981*, pages 1-56 (1984)
1980-1984	Mancetter Fort, Sites 3A & 3B, the West Defences
1980-1984	Mancetter Fort, Site 5, the Manor Kitchen Garden
1981-1982	Mancetter Fort, Site 6, Mancetter Farm:farmyard
1982	Sites 3A – 7 above: Scott, K.,'Mancetter Village: a 1st century fortress continued', B.W.A.S., Vol.102, *Transactions for 1998*, pages 1 – 55 (2000)
1988	Mancetter Fort, Site 11, Mancetter parish church car park
	Scott, K., W.M.A., notes in Vol. 31,
1989	Roman building, Witherley Apparently unpublished. But see report by John Ellis in the

Heartland Evening News, 23rd August 1997, entitled 'Keith's best find of his life', followed by another, 12th Sept 1997: 'Historic discovery led to site shut down'

1990   Home Close, Mancetter, Riding Arena Site (unpublished)

1989-1990   Mancetter Fort, Site 8, the South Defences

Scott, K,. W.M.A., notes in Vols. 32, 33, 34,

1992-1996   Mancetter Fort, Site 9, Mill Lane

Scott, K., W.M.A., notes in Vols. 37 and 39,

1993-1994   The Witherley Lodge site
Melton, N.D.,'Excavations at Witherley Lodge, Witherley, 1993-1994,' B.W.A.S., Vol .112, *Transactions for 2008*, pages 33-43 (2008)

1996-1997   Mancetter Fort, Site 10, the North Defences

Scott, K., W.M.A., notes in Vol. 40.

POST-ROMAN SITES

1967-1971   Medieval pottery kilns, Chilvers Coton

Mayes, P. And Scott, K. 1984. Pottery kilns at Chilvers Coton, Nuneaton. The Society for Medieval Archaeology Monograph Series, 10. London: Society for Medieval Archaeology

1974   Church End, Ansley

Melton,N.D. 2006. 'A late eighteenth-century

clearance .....from Church End, Ansley, Warwickshire,' *Transactions of the Birmingham and Warwickshire Archaeological Society*, Vol. 109, pages 85-96.

1979   18th century brick kiln, at 9, Witherley Road, Atherstone

Scott, K, and Ory, M. 1980. 'Brick making in North Warwickshire.'. *Transactions of the Birmingham and Warwickshire Archaeological Society*, Vol 89, pages 137-144.

1979   'Medieval building at 35, Old Forge Road, Fenny Drayton, Leicestershire.'

Scott, K. 1980. Medieval building at 35, Old Forge Road, Fenny Drayton, Leicestershire. *Transactions of the Leicestershire Archaeological and Historical Society*, Vol 54, pages 71-74.

1986   'Polesworth: a North Warwickshire country pottery,'

Melton, N. and Scott, K. 1999. 'Polesworth: a North Warwickshire country pottery,' *Post Medieval Archaeology*, Vol 33, pages 4-126.

APPENDIX 5 - FURTHER READING

The Annals of Imperial Rome and the Agricola of Tacitus, and the Histories of Dio Cassius, are all available in modern translation, and are well worth the attention of those interested in the subject of this book. Unhelpfully, neither writer gives the slightest clue as to the whereabouts of the final battle!

Among much published modern material the following are recommended:

Salway, P. (1991) *Roman Britain* Oxford University Press
Probably the best general account of Britain as part of the Roman Empire available.

Crummy, P. (1997) *City of Victory* Colchester Archaeological Trust
The story of Colchester, Britain's first Roman town; in particular, it contains all the latest archaeological evidence.

Webster, G., ed. (1988) *Fortress into City* Batsford
A major work containing papers by six archaeologists relating to the consolidation of Roman Britain in the first Century AD and the story of how six cities developed from earlier fortresses.

Webster,G. (1969;3rd Edition 1985) *The Roman Imperial Army*
A&C Black
The title says it all. A valuable work covering the legions, the auxiliaries, and the navy; their equipment and organisation.

Peddie, J. (1997; 2005) *Conquest – The Roman Invasion of Britain* St Martin's Press
Particularly informative in regards to the logistics of army supply organisation.

Selkirk, R. (1995) *On the Trail of the Legions*
Anglia Publishing
Also most useful for an understanding of the supply services and communications.

Cottrell, L (1969) *The Great Invasion* Macmillan

Shire Publications have a large range of booklets relating to the archaeology and history of Ancient Britain. Many cover Roman sites and events, and also specialised subjects. They are published under the general title of "Shire Archaeology" and are widely available. I recommend:-

Sealey, P.	*The Boudican Revolt Against Rome*
de La Bedoyere, G.	*Samian War*
Swann, V.	*Pottery in Roman Britain*
Webster, G.	*Boudica: the British Revolt against Rome AD60* (London, first published 1978, reprinted 2003)
Casey, P. J.	*Roman Coinage in Britain*

OTHER ARCHAEOLOGICAL REFERENCES[25]

O'Neill, StJohn Bryan H. *Excavation At Mancetter,* 1927, *Transactions of the Birmingham Archaeological Society*, Vol. 53 (1928), pages 173-195.

Oswald, A., 'A hoard of Roman coins from Mancetter,' *Transactions of Birmingham and Warwickshire Archaeological Society*, Vol. 79 (1960-1) pages 117-120.

Oswald, A. & Gathercole, P.W., 'Observation and excavation at Manduessedum, 1954-6,' *Transactions of the Birmingham and WarwickshireArchaeological Society*, Vol. 74, (1956), pages 30-52.

Mahany, C., 'Excavations at Manduessedum, 1964,' *Transactions of the Birmingham and Warwickshire Archaeological Society*, Vol. 84 (1967-70), pages 18 - 44.

Baddeley, C. , 'Mancetter', *Current Archaeology*, Vol. 125 (1991), pages -214.

---

[25]Added by editors

ACKNOWLEDGEMENTS

Any work of this type, by its very nature, relies on information gained from many sources, but first of all tribute must be paid to Keith Scott and the team of excavators who worked with him over the years. The site maps and plans provided by Keith all appeared in his excavation reports or were hand-outs for parties taken on the Society's 'Roman Trail'.

I am most grateful to Mrs. Kay Hartley for her many kindnesses in relation to my account of the Mancetter-Hartshill pottery industry. My thanks also to the late Ms. Vivien Swan for her permission to reproduce the pottery kiln drawings which appeared in her book "The Pottery Kilns of Roman Britain". These illustrations help in visualising the scene when visiting the Broad Close field site. I am immensely grateful to Kate Clarke who worked so hard in producing all the other drawings, plans and illustrations which form an essential part of this account. Kate coped uncomplainingly with the demands involved.

The late Dr. Graham Webster was tutor and mentor of so many archaeologists, both professional and amateur, post World War II, via his excavations and courses. He encouraged the use of minds and skills and was always ready to assist with advice. It gives me much pleasure to record my own thanks for this in the encouragement I received when commencing the original draft of this project, in particular regarding the Boudican revolt and its relation to the details of my thoughts on the Mancetter battlefield site.

He also much approved the insertion of the chapter on the organisation of the Roman army. Dr Webster was, of course, one of the country's leading authorities on the subject.

I also wish to thank Dr. Roger White and Timothy Strickland for helpful information when I was preparing earlier drafts of the manuscript; needless to say any errors and wrong conclusions are solely my responsibility. Finally, I must express my gratitude to Philip Taylor and his wife, Maria, for the massive amount of work they have undertaken in producing the typescripts through several stages, bearing with my additions and alterations until we reached its final form.

I would like to record here my gratitude for the cooperation and tolerance of the various land owners without whom none of this work could have been carried out.

Colin Baddeley

PHOTOGRAPHIC CREDITS

Many of the excavation photographs were provided by
Keith Scott and the remainder were taken by myself. All the
finds photographs are Keith's.

In regard to the air photographs, that of the *burgus* area is
published by kind permission of the Cambridge University
Collection of Air Photographs. The other has been provided
by the late Jim Pickering, an independent air archaeologist
who made a huge and most important contribution to our
knowledge of sites, especially the existence of hundreds of
previously unknown sites in the Midlands and elsewhere.

Grateful acknowledgements are due to The Friends of
Atherstone Heritage for permission to use their computer-
developed pictures of the half-legionary fortress at
Mancetter, prepared by Richard Haigh
(image above and on page 36).

C.B